Hello!
I am a panda.

China is the only place where pandas live in the wild.

Pandas live in cool, misty mountain forests.
It's like having a cozy tree house in the clouds!

Pandas live in cozy dens or hollow trees in bamboo forests.

The black and white fur helps pandas blend into their bamboo forest homes.

Pandas' size and strength help protect them.

We don't have many natural predators, but we need to be careful of snow leopards and wild dogs.

An adult panda can weigh as much as 300 pounds (136kg).

Pandas stand about 4 to 6 feet (1.6m) tall.

Pandas are mostly vegetarian and eat bamboo.

Pandas are "omnivores" because they sometimes eat small animals or birds.

Pandas can sleep for about 10 to 16 hours a day.
Is it "panda bedtime" yet?

I'm an expert napper.

Pandas may look slow, but they can run as fast as 20 miles (32km) per hour!

Even though pandas can run, they are usually slow and steady.

Pandas are not great swimmers.

Unlike some other animals, we don't spend a lot of time in the water. We prefer staying on dry land and munching on bamboo.

Pandas have an incredible sense of smell.

A panda's sense of smell is so good that they can smell bamboo from miles away.

Pandas have good hearing.

A panda's keen sense of hearing helps them be aware of what's around them and avoid danger.

Pandas are usually "solitary" animals. That means they like to live alone.

Pandas sometimes share their territory with other pandas, but...

Pandas don’t form herds or groups like other animals.

Pandas make noises like honks and growls.

Each sound means something different, like saying "hello," asking for attention, or telling others they're ready to find a panda partner.

Pandas show affection by playing together.
We like having panda playdates!

Pandas use body language, like standing on their hind legs or rolling on the ground.

Panda cubs stay with their moms for their first couple of years.

Pandas like to stay in their home territory and only explore nearby.

Sometimes pandas may roam around, but they don't go on long journeys.

There are fewer than 2000 pandas in the world.

Pandas can live up to 20 years in the wild, and even longer in captivity.
I get to celebrate 20 birthdays!

I am a panda.
Goodbye!

Want more?

... and more

COLLECT THEM ALL!

ActiveBrainsBooks.com

Hello parents!

Visit us to find out about new releases and ***FREE*** offers. We'll let you know when we have a new release coming out and how you can get it for FREE.
And you can cast your vote for what book we make next!

ActiveBrainsBooks.com

or visit here

scan here

Let us know what you think. As an independent publisher, your honest reviews mean a lot to us and our business. We'd love to hear from you!

amazon.com/review/create-review/

on Amazon.

amazon.com/author/activebrainsbooks

ActiveBrainsBooks.com

www.ingramcontent.com/pod-product-compliance
Lightning Source LLC
LaVergne TN
LVHW070224110826
845147LV00003B/637

* 9 7 8 1 9 5 7 3 3 7 7 3 9 *